THIS BOOK BELONGS TO:

_____

WELCOME TO KANSAS

Dedicated to all the explorers.

All rights reserved.
No part of this book may be reproduced in any form or by any means, electronic or mechanical, and no photocopying or recording, unless you have written permission from the author.

ISBN 978-1-958985-77-9

Text copyright © 2025 by Mimi Jones

www.joeysavestheday.com

A Mimi Book

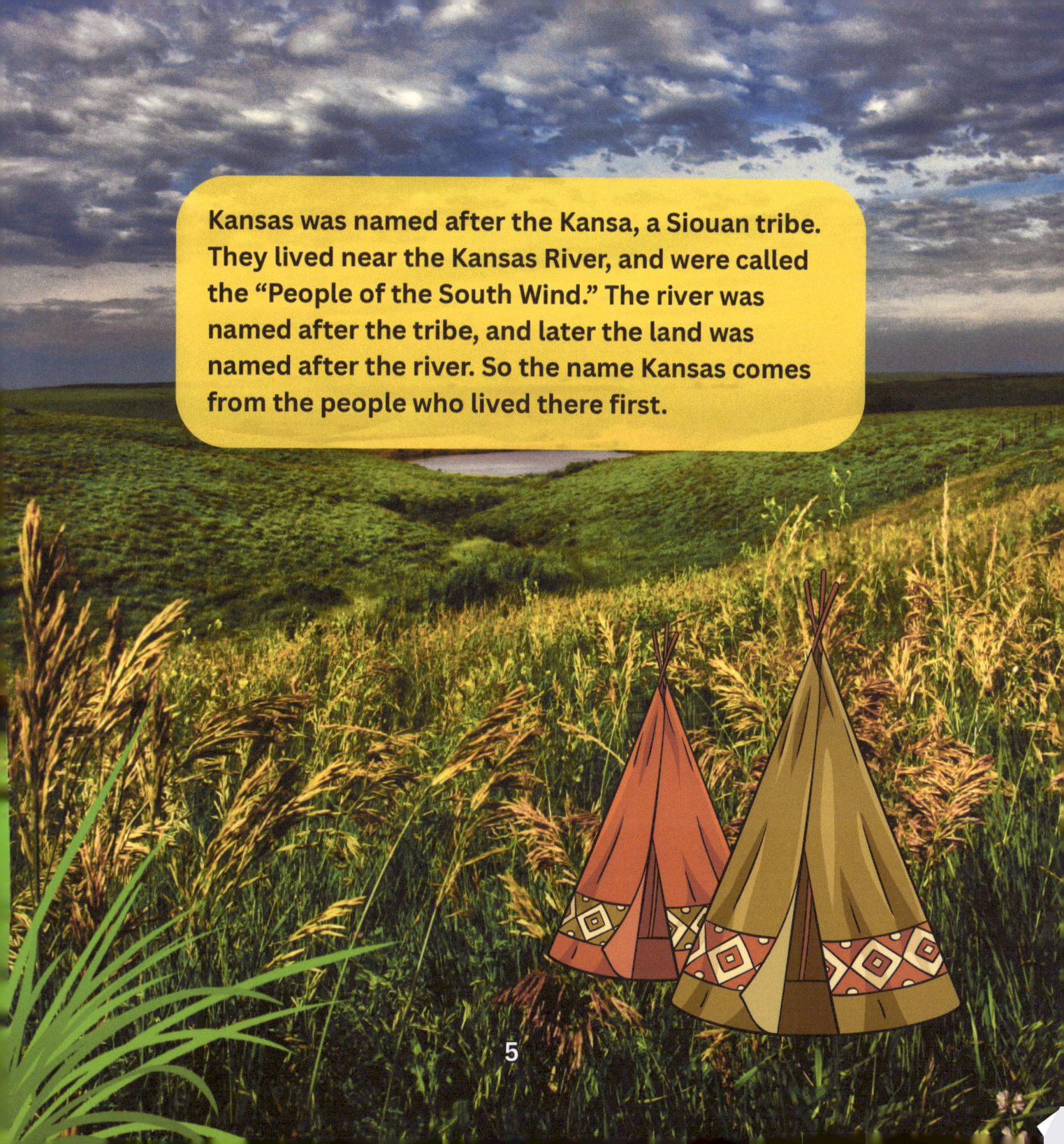

Kansas was named after the Kansa, a Siouan tribe. They lived near the Kansas River, and were called the "People of the South Wind." The river was named after the tribe, and later the land was named after the river. So the name Kansas comes from the people who lived there first.

Kansas was the thirty-fourth state to join the Union. It officially joined on January 29, 1861.

Kansas is bordered by four states: Colorado, Nebraska, Missouri, and Oklahoma.

Topeka is the capital of Kansas.
It officially became the capital in 1861.

Topeka, Kansas, has an estimated population of about 125,467 people.

Kansas State Capital Building

Kansas is the fifteenth largest state in the U.S., covering 82,278 square miles, showcasing a diverse landscape that includes rolling plains, expansive prairies, and picturesque rivers.

There are about 2,919,179 people who live in the state of Kansas.

Amelia Earhart, born in Atchison, Kansas, was the first woman to fly solo across the Atlantic Ocean. She was a brave aviator and a talented author who inspired people all over the world with her achievements.

Wichita, Kansas, is sometimes called the "Air Capital of the World" because of how many airplane manufacturers are based there.

Kansas

There are 105 counties in Kansas.

Here is a list of twenty of those counties:

Barber	Rawlins	Butler	Haskell
Crawford	Meade	Atchison	Kiowa
Harper	Russell	Cherokee	Marshall
Ellis	Wichita	Finney	Miami
Jewell	Clay	Greeley	Pratt

Monument Rocks, also known as the Chalk Pyramids, is a National Natural Landmark located in western Kansas. These impressive formations are made of chalk and rise dramatically from the flat plains.

KANSAS

The Oregon Trail was a path used by pioneers in the 1800s to move west to Oregon. One of the states It went through was Kansas, where travelers crossed flat lands and faced tough weather.

Kansas' state tree is the Cottonwood Tree.

The Overland Park Arboretum is a big park in Kansas with gardens, trails, and fun places to explore. You can see butterflies, flowers, and learn about plants from around the world.

The Kansas state bird is the Western Meadowlark. It was chosen as the state bird in 1937.

The official Kansas state flower is the Wild Sunflower. It was chosen as the state flower in 1897.

The official nickname for Kansas is "The Sunflower State," but it also has several other nicknames such as "The Jayhawker State."

 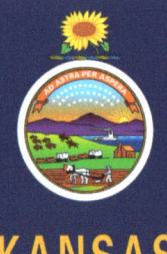 

The Kansas state motto, "Ad astra per aspera," translates to "to the stars through difficulties" and embodies the resilience and determination of its residents. The motto was officially adopted on May 25, 1861.

 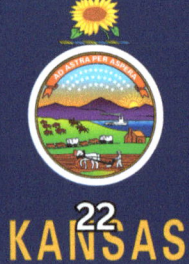 

The abbreviation for Kansas is KS.

KS

The Kansas state flag was officially adopted on March 23, 1927.

Some crops grown in Kansas are corn, millet, soybeans, and wheat.

Some animals that live in Kansas are bats, chipmunks, deer, foxes, and rabbits.

Kansas can get very hot and cold depending on the time of year. The hottest temperature recorded was 121 degrees Fahrenheit in Fredonia on July 18, 1936, and the lowest was -40 degrees Fahrenheit in Lebanon on February 13, 1905.

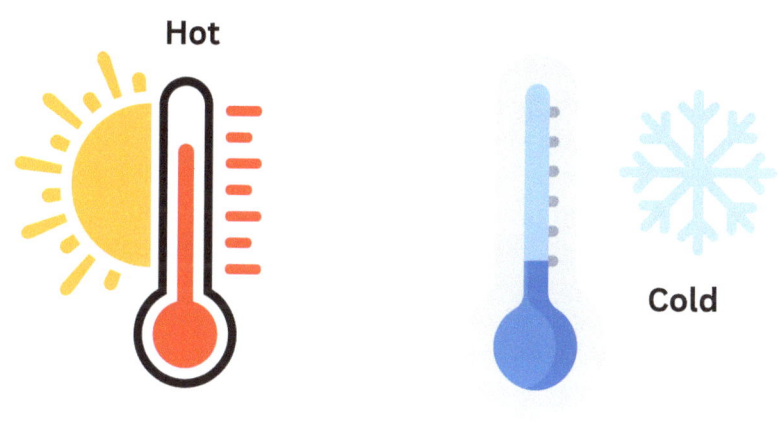

Pizza Hut was founded in 1958 in Wichita, Kansas by two college brothers, Dan and Frank Carney. They borrowed $600 from their mom and opened a small pizza shop near campus. Their tasty pizza quickly became popular, and that little shop grew into one of the biggest pizza chains in the world—all starting right in Kansas!

Susanna M. Salter was the first woman elected mayor in the United States. In 1887, she won the election in Argonia, Kansas, even though her name was put on the ballot as a joke! She proved women could lead with strength and kindness.

Wichita Dwight D. Eisenhower National Airport is the biggest airport in Kansas. It's named after President Dwight D. Eisenhower, who grew up in Kansas. The airport helps people fly to cities like Denver, Chicago, and Orlando. It has a shiny new terminal and lots of space for airplanes.

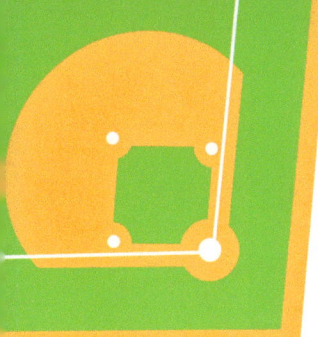

The Kansas City Royals, based in Kansas City, Missouri, are a Major League Baseball team established in 1969. They compete in the American League Central Division and play their home games at Kauffman Stadium, known for its iconic fountains and fan-friendly atmosphere. The Royals have a proud history, highlighted by multiple World Series appearances and championship wins.

The Kansas City Chiefs, based in Kansas City, Missouri, are a professional NFL team founded in 1960. They play their home games at GEHA Field at Arrowhead Stadium. The Chiefs are celebrated for their rich legacy, including multiple Super Bowl victories, and a passionate fan base known for their sea of red and unmatched energy on game day.

ZOO

Sedgwick County Zoo in Wichita, Kansas is the largest zoo in the state and home to over 3,000 animals from around the world. Some of the animals living here include elephants, gorillas, lions, and giraffes!

Wilson State Park is a beautiful place in central Kansas with clear water, rocky hills, and lots of outdoor fun.

Families can swim, fish, hike, and camp near Wilson Lake, which is known as the clearest lake in the state.

I hope you enjoyed learning about Kansas.

To explore fun facts about the other 49 states, visit my website at www.joeysavestheday.com. You'll also find a wide variety of homeschool resources to support joyful learning at home. If you enjoyed this book, I would be grateful if you left a review. Your feedback truly helps. Thank you for your support!

Check out these other interesting books in the
50 States Fact Books Series!

www.mimibooks.com

www.ingramcontent.com/pod-product-compliance
Lightning Source LLC
Chambersburg PA
CBHW040027050426
42453CB00002B/37